A POCKET C▮▮▮▮▮▮

D1362497

CORNWALL

Introduction

If visitors to Cornwall were asked what they like about the county, there would undoubtedly be a very long list, for the great attraction of this south-westerly tip of England is its tremendous variety. The magnificent coastline has some of the most dramatic cliff scenery in Britain, broken by tiny coves and fascinating little fishing villages. At other points along the coast stretch immense expanses of sandy beach backed by rolling dunes. Inland, windswept moorland is adorned by strange rock formations sculpted by the elements, and by the stone relics left by prehistoric man. The sheltered southern river estuaries have woods coming down to the shore, where countless yachts and dinghies sit bobbing at anchor when the tide is high, or lie exposed and stranded on the mud-flats waiting for the return of the water. The west of the county is littered with the remains of the old tin-mining industry; gaunt chimney-stacks emerging from ruined engine-houses. And, throughout the countryside, narrow lanes criss-cross their way between towns and villages, bounded by high Cornish hedges which are, in fact, dry stone walls covered by earth and a profusion of wild flowers. Cornish walls are a delight to the eye, with their traditional herring-bone patterns still being produced today.

Apart from the beauty of the countryside and seashore, Cornwall has much to offer in the way of facilities, entertainment and interesting places to visit.

Mevagissey

Accommodation is available in most areas, although it becomes well booked during the summer season. Holiday centres such as Bude, Newquay, Penzance and Falmouth provide organised entertainment and all kinds of sports facilities. Sea- and freshwater angling are popular along much of the coast and on some of the rivers. Cornwall's beaches, with their soft golden sand, offer the traditional seaside holiday; not only are there zoos, craft centres, miniature railways and theme and wildlife parks to provide entertainment, but the county has a unique heritage which manifests itself to the discerning visitor in a variety of ways. The villages and towns, with their ancient churches, enshrine the past, and castles, stately homes, beautiful gardens containing many rare species of shrubs and plants, museums, prehistoric remains and industrial archaeology add an additional dimension.

This book attempts to give a taste of the many sides of Cornwall: its history, legends and language; the local food, drink and industries; an introduction to places to visit; and a brief glimpse of the wildlife and Cornwall's natural beauty. At the end, a gazetteer is included, with short descriptions of many of the towns and villages, and mention of near-by attractions.

The map on pages 60–62 gives the locations of places of interest mentioned in the book. Numbers and grid references shown against items in the text refer to this map.

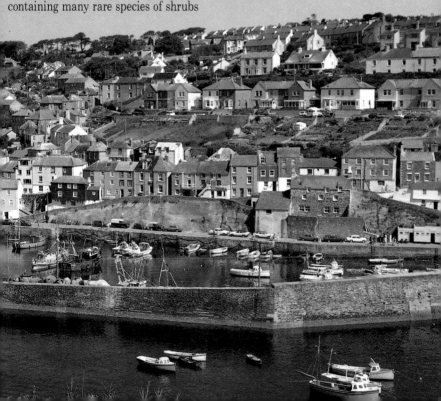

History

Cornwall's early history is shrouded in mystery and legend, but archaeological finds show that man has occupied this peninsula since prehistoric times, probably attracted by the mineral wealth, fishing and mild climate. Early records show that the Phoenicians visited here to trade for tin. Later, the Romans came and left without making too much impression on this isolated corner, and then, like the rest of England, Cornwall retreated into obscurity for several centuries. It was during this period that the spread of Christianity to Britain began. Celtic saints landed in Cornwall from Brittany, Ireland and Wales, which were other strongholds of the Celtic language and traditions. We are still reminded of these early missionaries through place-names and by the wealth of Celtic stone crosses and holy wells to be found in the county.

By about AD 600 Anglo-Saxons were spreading their influence across the country, and it is probably their clashes with a powerful local chieftain that have formed the basis of the stories of King Arthur and his court. The Saxons finally established themselves, only to be ousted by the Normans under William the Conqueror.

The Normans built castles at strategic points, such as Launceston and Lostwithiel, and developed the local tin-mining industry, which was one of the mainstays of the economy until the end of the nineteenth century. The mines

Royal Albert Bridge, Saltash

were administered by stannary courts, which were a form of local parliament. The independent-minded Cornish have often rebelled against central government: they objected to Henry VII's heavy taxes and tried to resist the introduction of the New English Prayer Book in Edward VI's reign. But their fighting spirit was invaluable to England during Elizabeth I's war with Spain in the late sixteenth century, when sea battles took place off the Cornish coast and Cornish privateers raided Spanish vessels.

Cornwall was a divided county during the Civil War, and fierce battles took place at Stamford Hill, Braddock Down and Tresillian Bridge. Royalist strongholds in the county finally capitulated in 1645. A century later saw the growth of the Methodist tradition in Cornwall. The brothers John and Charles Wesley led the religious revival which was to take a strong hold on the working people of the county. Chapels sprang up in many villages and thousands flocked to hear the brothers preach. This was the period when, despite the opposition of the Methodists, the smuggling trade was at its height. To the impoverished Cornish this was a necessary way of life, for mining, fishing and agriculture did not bring in good wages, and smuggling flourished until well into the nineteenth century.

In 1859 a new era dawned for Cornwall with the opening of Brunel's mighty railway bridge over the River Tamar at Saltash. The isolated peninsula became linked with the rest of the country and, by the turn of the century, it was becoming a fashionable place to visit. This role has expanded and the county is now one of the most popular English holiday areas for visitors from all over the world.

Prehistoric monuments

The countryside of Cornwall is richly endowed with relics of its ancient past. The land abounds in chambered tombs and barrows or burial mounds, stone circles and standing stones, quoits and cromlechs, Iron Age forts and settlements. Owing to the relatively undeveloped nature of Cornwall, many are in a good state of preservation, especially in the Penwith Peninsula and on Bodmin Moor. Undoubtedly local superstition prevented many stone monuments from being pillaged by local people for building materials.

The Hurlers, Bodmin Moor

Just off the A30, about 7m. NE of Bodmin, *(1)* the **Stripple Stones** (map ref. H21) can be seen to the north on Hawkstor Downs. Similar to Stonehenge in Wiltshire, these standing stones form a circle and were probably the site of some pagan ritual. They are enclosed by a ditch and earthen bank. Over twenty unenclosed circles remain, the most impressive of which are probably *(2)* the **Hurlers** (J23), composed of three separate stone circles in a line. They are located on Bodmin Moor, due east of Siblyback Reservoir, and can be reached by a track leading to the north-west out of Minions. This whole area is rich in prehistoric remains.

An easily accessible circle, *(3)* the **Merry Maidens** (J4), lies on the south side of the B3315 coast road from Penzance to Land's End, 1m. W of the road down to Lamorna. Two four-metre (fourteen-foot) standing stones known as *(4)* the **Pipers** (J4) can be seen to the north-east of the circle, across the main road. Cornish folklore maintains that the Merry Maidens and the Pipers were

turned to stone as a punishment for merrymaking on the Sabbath.

Dozens of other large Bronze Age standing stones are scattered across Cornwall, like isolated sentinels guarding fields and moorland. They may have served as gravestones or to mark some significant event, but it is unlikely that we shall ever know their actual function.

The early inhabitants of Cornwall had another impressive way of housing their dead. Huge granite slabs were stood up like a stone card-house and covered with a capstone or quoit for a roof. The whole structure was then covered by earth. Wind and excavations have now removed the earth and we are able to see the original stone chambers. Excellent examples are: *(5)* **Trethevy Quoit** (K23), north of Liskeard between Tremar and Darite; *(6)* **Chun Quoit**

**Lanyon Quoit,
Penwith Peninsula**

(H4), about ¾m. S of Morvah (very well preserved); *(7)* **Lanyon Quoit** (I4), half-way along the Penzance to Morvah road on the right; and *(8)* **Zennor Quoit** (H6), 2m. SE of the village on a hill (cremated bones, pottery and tools were found in this tomb). European chamber tombs often had a stone with a hole in it at the entrance, presumably to help seal the tomb, but allowing passage for additional bodies. In Cornwall, *(9)* the **Men-an-Tol** (H4) is perhaps one of these, but it is not located near an actual tomb. Instead it lies between two upright stones about ½m. N of Lanyon Quoit, off the Penzance to Morvah road. Local superstition claims that ailments can be cured if the sufferer is passed through the hole. The third millenium chambered tomb at Tregiffian near St Buryan, not far from the Merry Maidens, is also an impressive sepulchral relic.

The Iron Age Celtic people who came to Britain about the sixth century BC left some fascinating reminders of their life-style, of which Cornwall has many. The increase in population meant a shortage of land, and strategic hill-tops were fortified with concentric rings of earth-works and defended with slingstones and other more sophisticated weapons. *(10)* **Castle-an-Dinas** (H17), about 1½m. SE of St Columb Major, and *(11)* **Carn Brea** (J10), 1m. SW of Redruth, are examples of such hill forts and settle-ments and give a good idea of the fortifications and buildings of these new inhabitants. Many cliff-top promon-tories were also fortified by ditches and banks, such as at Gurnard's Head, Rumps Point and Trevelgue (north of

Men-an-Tol, Penwith Peninsula

Newquay). The Iron Age fort of *(12)* **Castle Dore** (K19), on the B3269 2m. NW of Fowey, was reoccupied in the sixth century AD by King Mark of Cornwall, father of Tristan. The legend of the tragic lovers Tristan and Isolde is commemorated by a near-by stone.

But to return to the Iron Age, an early cemetery has been found at *(13)* **Harlyn Bay** (E17), west of Padstow, containing many stone coffins.

By about the first century AD larger unfortified villages were built. Excavations at *(14)* **Chysauster** (I5), on the Penwith Peninsula, have unearthed a remarkably well-preserved village 'street', with four houses each side. Behind, walled fields indicate the beginnings of cultivation. Nearby is a fougou, an underground chamber, examples of which are often found in these settlements. Their function is not known, but guesses range from hiding-places to larders. The village is maintained by English Heritage and is a fascinating place to visit.

Even better-preserved fougous can be seen at *(15)* **Carn Euny** (I4) (near Sancreed, west of Penzance), where underground chambers fifteen metres (fifty feet) long are lined by stone blocks, with slabs of granite for the roof. These are also maintained by English Heritage.

Legends

Many people, both visitors and locals alike, will scoff at the legends and superstitions of Cornish folklore. But the old legends make splendid tales, and many of the superstitions are linked with stories which defy explanation. Well into the nineteenth century there was widespread belief in witches, healing charms, fairies and other spirit peoples, and a few traces of these old beliefs undoubtedly remain today. Fear of the Devil was such that houses were sometimes built in the round so that the Devil could find no corners in which to hide. Examples can still be seen at Veryan, east of Falmouth.

The legend of King Arthur and his Knights of the Round Table has been immortalised by such varied talents as Tennyson and Walt Disney, and numerous places in Cornwall stake their claim to some association with this well-loved monarch. Tintagel retains its hold on the public imagination, and indeed offers a wealth of information about the legend, but scholars doubt its authenticity as the site of Arthur's castle. Dozmary Pool on Bodmin Moor claims to be the spot where King Arthur's sword, Excalibur,

The coast near Zennor

Tintagel Castle

was thrown after his death, and seized by a ghostly hand which drew it beneath the water. (This event has also been attributed to Loe Pool near Helston.) Dozmary Pool is also renowned as the place where the wicked Jan Tregeagle was sentenced by the Devil, to whom he had sold his soul, to empty the pool with a leaky limpet-shell.

The moors can still be treacherous, particularly in bad weather, and the unwary can get into difficulties with the bogs and rock-strewn uplands. So when you walk across the moors to climb Rough Tor and Brown Willy, the two main moorland peaks, take care not to be pisky-led, for these mischievous little people are reputed to lead unfortunate travellers round and round in circles for hours on end!

Other elfin-like people, known as 'knackers', inhabited the mines. They were generally a lucky omen, for they were usually associated with rich lodes and could be heard tapping away with their tiny hammers. But to be on the safe side, miners would leave a piece of their lunch to keep the knackers happy.

A well-known legend from the Penwith Peninsula originates in Zennor. Here a mermaid was attracted by the singing of one Matthew Trewhella, who was in the church choir. She enticed him out with her own beautiful singing and they disappeared together beneath the waves. The event is recorded by a magnificently carved bench-end in the church. Also vanished beneath the sea is the lost land of Lyonesse, which used to lie between Land's End and the Scilly Isles.

The Cornish language

The Celtic people of the south-western tip of Britain managed to resist the spread of the English language and culture for over ten centuries. They remained an isolated tribe with their own language and customs. Other Celtic tribes survived in Wales and in Brittany, and modern Cornish-speakers can be understood quite well by speakers of Welsh or Breton. The latter two languages have continued in use, whereas by the end of the eighteenth century the Cornish language had finally disappeared from everyday speech under the strong influence of English and the refusal of the authorities to translate the New Prayer Book into Cornish.

At Paul, near Penzance, stands a memorial to Dolly Pentreath, who died in 1777 and was reputed to be the last speaker of Cornish, although she was probably the last person to refuse to speak English. Her monument is inscribed in Cornish, and throughout the Duchy are other native signs and inscriptions. A Cornish version of the Lord's Prayer is often displayed in churches.

Common words

als, owles: cliff
bal: mine
bos: home, dwelling
bre, brea: hill
carn: rock pile
carrek, carrick: rock
chy: house
cum, combe: small valley
dowr, dour: water
du, dhu: black, dark
dynas, dennis: castle
eglos: church
enys, ennis: island
foss, vose: wall
glas, glaze: green, blue
gun, goon, noon: moor, plain
hal, hale: downland
Kernow, Curnow: Cornwall
melyn: mill
men, maen: stone
meynek, minack: stony
mor: sea
nans, nant: valley
pen, pedn: headland
plen an gwary: open-air theatre
pol, poll: pool
pons, ponds, pont: bridge
porth: cover, harbour
res, red, ret: ford
ros, rose: peninsula
sans, sant: holy
scath: boat
towan: sandhill
tre, tref: farm, town, settlement
treth, treath: beach, ferry
wheal, whel: mine

Place-names

Coverack: little streams
Hayle: estuary
Kynance: ravine
Looe: inlet
Marazion: little market
Pentire: headland
Penzance: holy head
Poldhu: black pool
Porthpean: little beach
Redruth: red ford
Trewint: windy farm

Although not yet an annual event, the Cornish Eisteddfod is a celebration of Cornwall's unique culture.

Even though Cornish has not been the widespread spoken language since the sixteenth century, it has lingered on in thousands of place-names and in surnames. Certain prefixes are extremely common, as illustrated by the old rhyme:

By Tre, Ros, Pol, Lan, Car and Pen
Ye shall know most Cornishmen.

The list opposite covers some common Cornish words, many of which are incorporated in the names of towns, villages, streets, rivers and hills. The second list gives translations of some Cornish place-names.

Dolly Pentreath's memorial at Paul

In the early twentieth century a movement started to revive the language and this has been gaining considerable momentum in recent years. A number of very young children are now taught to speak the language as a 'mother-tongue', classes are held throughout the county and some schools include Cornish in their curriculum. The study of the language is encouraged by the Cornish Language Board and the Cornish Gorsedd, a college of bards whose aims include the furtherance of all matters truly Cornish in origin – traditions, history, language, literature, poetry, music and the like.

Industry

Cornwall has never been a heavily industrialised county, but while this has helped preserve the natural beauty of the region, it has also meant hardship in terms of lack of employment. Tin and copper mining were major industries in the seventeenth to nineteenth centuries, but have since almost completely died out, the closure of the mine at Geevor in 1986 being yet another blow to the already ailing industry. Fishing and shipbuilding were once important economic activities but are now continued on a much smaller scale. Tourism is now second only to agriculture as the county's main industry, with the production and exporting of china clay of considerable economic importance. Cornwall has also become well known for its slate and granite quarries, which have provided material for many famous buildings.

Mining

Mining has been of great importance in Cornwall since before the Roman occupation of Britain, for the tin, copper and lead found here were valuable for trade. The tin-miners became so powerful that, after the Norman Conquest, a Royal Charter divided Cornwall into four stannary districts based on the mines, with their own laws, courts and parliament. Under Elizabeth I four stannary or coinage towns were established, where tin ingots were brought. The corners were chopped off and tested and the value of the tin was then stamped on the block. The French word for corner is *coin*, hence our words 'coin' and 'coinage'.

The working conditions of the early tin-miners were quite intolerable.

Crown's Mine, Botallack

Primitive tools, poor ventilation, feeble candlelight and badly shored-up shafts only exaggerated the dangers of what is still a very hazardous profession. Miserable wages meant food was always scarce, making miners and their families prone to ill-health.

The early mine-workings tended to be shallow because of the problems of drainage, but the arrival of the steam engine and pump in the late eighteenth century radically changed the situation. The powerful new machines could pump out water from great depths, provide the energy to lift men and materials, and could be used to crush and separate the rock and ore. This last job was previously done by young boys and women – the latter known as 'bal maidens'. Richard Trevithick, born in Camborne in 1771, did much to develop the early steam-engines. A statue of him can be found outside Camborne Library. Another Cornish inventor, Sir Humphry Davy, from Penzance, was responsible for the

miners' safety-lamp, which he produced in 1815. This not only provided a more reliable light, but also gave warning of the presence of dangerous gases. The Davy-lamp still serves that function today. The development of drills saved the laborious task of hammering out holes in which to place gunpowder charges.

The technological advances of the eighteenth and nineteenth centuries brought about a boom in the mining industry, but it was to be relatively short-lived, for cheaper production methods in other countries gradually forced the closure of Cornish mines. The present-day landscape is dotted with the stark ruins of engine-houses, their roofs gone and their crumbling brickwork choked with ivy.

The main mining area was around Redruth–Camborne and down the north coast to St Just. Many workings went out under the sea, such as Botallack Mine, which stretched a third of a mile under the Atlantic, and Levant Mine, part of which eventually gave in to the pressure of the ocean and flooded in 1930. As a result of a slump in world tin prices, two of Cornwall's famous mines, Geevor at Pendeen and Wheal Pendarves at Camborne, have now closed. However, South Crofty Mine at Illogan is still working and two new mines, Wheal Jane and Mount Wellington, in the Carnon Valley on the outskirts of Truro, are also in operation. All three can be visited by prior arrangement with the management.

Another method of obtaining tin was by 'streaming', a process which used water-power to crush the ore and separate out the tin oxide. Apart from the hundreds of disused engine-houses visible in the county, visitors may also like to see more of the old mining technology. Many local museums have

Towanroath Shaft, Wheal Coates Mine, St Agnes

13

sections on industrial history and the National Trust owns two massive beam-engines at Pool. New technology has also come to Cornwall in the shape of the Camborne School of Mines Geothermal Energy Project, a government-sponsored research programme to investigate 'hot rocks', an exciting new option for electricity generation. In such ways new industry could replace the old.

China clay

The newcomer to Cornwall may be surprised to see steep white or grass-covered hills around St Austell. Closer inspection will reveal huge mounds of powder which is the waste material from the excavation of china clay, or kaolin as it is also called. The land and streams around St Austell are milky white with the deposits and in certain lights tongues of opaque turquoise stretch out into the sea, formed by reflection from the particles.

China-clay winning is a major Cornish industry and the produce is exported throughout the world. It was in 1755 that a Plymouth chemist, William Cookworthy, discovered that the decomposed granite could be used to make porcelain, and the idea was developed by the Wedgwood brothers. The clay is now also used in the manufacture of textiles, paper, chemicals, cosmetics and paints.

It is possible to arrange a tour round a china-clay works by contacting the English China Clay Group at John Keay House, St Austell. The Wheal Martyn Museum at Carthew, near St Austell, contains a restored nineteenth-century clay works, and the nature trail has a view of an open clay pit. More details of this and other museums can be found on pages 46–8.

Cornishmen and the sea

For centuries the sea provided a livelihood for many Cornish people, not only through fishing, but also through more dubious activities, such as smuggling and scavenging from the remains of wrecked ships. Although there is absolutely no proof that ships were actually lured to their doom by false lights, there is no doubt that local people profited greatly from the many vessels that foundered on the dangerous coastline. Money, valuables, food, brandy, all manner of cargo and all moveable wood and fitments from the ships would be spirited ashore, much to the fury of the ship-owners. Such losses encouraged the establishment of lighthouses along the coast, often to the annoyance of local people, particularly the eighteenth- and nineteenth-century tin-miners, who took great delight in plundering wrecks and even stripping the surviving sailors of all their belongings.

Fortunately, such horrific tales are balanced by stories of the bravery of

Mending nets at Looe

The Huer's House, Newquay

Cornish folk in going to the aid of distressed ships and sailors. There are countless instances of dramatic rescues by lifeboat, breeches-buoy, or the use of rocket-fired lines. One of the most recent and poignant dramas is still fresh in the minds of those who were involved with the Penlee lifeboat, which was lost with all hands during a violent storm on the night of 19 December 1981, when attempting the rescue of the crew and passengers of the equally ill-fated *Union Star.* The first lifeboat station was founded at Padstow in 1827 and there are now eleven stations round the coast. At Bude, Lizard–Cadgwith, Newquay, Padstow, Port Isaac, St Agnes, St Ives and Sennen Cove the boats are housed onshore and can be visited by the public at certain times. The Falmouth, Fowey and Penlee lifeboats are moored off-shore.

Fishing is still an important means of support in Cornwall, although gone are the days of the huge pilchard shoals of the eighteenth and nineteenth centuries. These tiny sardine-like fish became the mainstay of the inshore fishermen of St Ives, Newquay, Mevagissey and Mount's Bay. Boats working in teams lowered their weighted seine-nets round a shoal, hanging from cork floats. The net was then drawn tighter until the fish could be scooped into the waiting boats and taken ashore. The catch was then given into the hands of the womenfolk in the fish cellars. Often working far into the night, they took the pilchards and laid them row upon row on the floor, each layer sprinkled with salt. This solid, oily mass of fish was left for a few weeks before being packed into barrels and pressed with heavy stones to extract the remains of the oil.

The largest haul of pilchards ever recorded took place at St Ives in 1868, when 5,600 hogsheads, or 16,500,000 fish, were taken by one seine. But by the early twentieth century the huge shoals had disappeared and the cry of the huer was no longer heard from the cliff-top. This man was stationed to watch for the reddish streak in the water which heralded the arrival of the shoals. At the first sign he shouted, 'Hevva, hevva!' (from the Cornish word for shoal: *hevsa*), and the men, women and children would pour out of the buildings. The huer signalled to the men in the boats the direction in which the fish were moving and indicated when to 'shoot' the seine-nets. These look-out men waited in small cliff-top shelters, and the one at Newquay can still be seen on the promontory to the west of Towan Sands.

Although the departure of the pilchards was a serious blow to the Cornish fishermen, offshore and deep-sea fishing fleets continue to operate out of ports such as Newlyn, St Ives, Mousehole, Padstow and Looe, and today these places are important centres for an industry which supports many Cornish people.

Smuggling

To the poverty-stricken Cornishmen of earlier centuries smuggling was a logical extension of the fishing trade, since they lived so conveniently near the Continent and were surrounded by secret landing-places. Nearly everyone, including mayors, magistrates and parsons, helped with the smuggling and nobody thought of it as a crime for, after all, they had paid for the goods in the first place. The easily secured towers of some strategically placed parish churches afforded splendid sanctuary for contraband.

The most popular goods included tobacco, tea, brandy, rum, silks and salt, and these were brought into nearly every cove and harbour, including the more important towns such as St Ives, which concentrated on luxury goods, and Polperro, which specialised in building fast boats capable of eluding the coastguard.

The Cornish smuggler or 'Fair Trader' was basically an honourable man, preferring to use cunning to violence, who 'though no doubt highly blamable for violating the laws of his country, is frequently incapable of violating those of natural justice and who would have been in every respect an excellent citizen had not the laws of his country made that a crime which Nature never meant to be so' (Adam Smith). The most renowned Cornish smuggler was John Carter, the 'King of Prussia', whom even the revenue men respected for his honesty and integrity. Carter ran the family smuggling business from Prussia Cove and he was helped by his brother Harry, who later became a popular Methodist preacher.

The great era of smuggling in Cornwall was roughly divided into two periods: 'Free Trade' and 'Scientific'; and the methods used in each differed drastically. During the Free Trade period, smuggling was carried on openly and the few preventive officers were usually only too happy to accept a bribe. The

Polperro

smuggled goods were landed on the beach and were then collected by crowds of local villagers, some armed with clubs and others wearing special harnesses designed to carry two tubs of spirit each. Horses were also 'borrowed' from farmers, who were later well rewarded, and when this contraband train passed through villages, the inhabitants would turn their faces to the wall so that they could truthfully say they had seen nothing.

Prussia Cove

This Golden Age of smuggling soon came to a close, however, for when the war with France ended in 1815, the Government suddenly had enough surplus men and ships to form an efficient preventive service. This was the start of the Scientific period, when the smugglers realised that they would have to match their wits against the excisemen if they were to survive. The methods they devised were certainly ingenious; the most popular being 'crop-sowing'. Smuggling boats would anchor offshore while the tubs, known as 'ankers', were fastened to a length of rope interspersed with heavy stones. When night fell, the tubs were dropped overboard at a prearranged spot and the next day some innocent-looking fishing-boats would

An attack by the Revenue Men, _c._ 1820

casually halt in the same position and, using special pronged hooks called 'creepers' or 'centipedes', draw up the tubs and conceal them under their nets. The coastguards soon became equally adept at 'creeping' and so the smugglers moved on to more sophisticated methods. Boats with ingenious false bottoms were built, tobacco was plaited inside ropes, spirits were hidden in water-tanks with false sides, and one captain went so far as to stuff a turkey with rare silks – it is hardly surprising that the preventive force was frequently baffled!

The preventive force, however, was growing stronger and more loyal all the time and it was this factor, coupled with a reduction of duties on goods, that finally led to the decline in smuggling in Cornwall. It had earlier been estimated that, if all the goods smuggled into Falmouth alone in the course of one year had been taxed, the money collected would have been more than twice the land tax for the whole kingdom but, with the risks increasing dramatically and the profits growing less, smuggling on a large scale ceased to be a viable proposition and gradually died a natural death.

Lighthouses

The rocky Cornish coast has always proved hazardous to shipping, particularly when combined with the extreme weather conditions that can blow up along this exposed Atlantic shore. From early times beacons were lit to warn shipping of local dangers and the Merchant Venturers of Bristol provided funds to repair the tower of St Eval Parish Church, which was a valuable aid to navigation. In the sixteenth century the mariners' guilds formed Trinity House, which is now the sole authority responsible for lighthouses and other navigational markers round the English coast.

Certain Cornish mainland lighthouses are open to the public free of charge from 1 pm to one hour before

Godrevy Island from Godrevy Point

Lizard Point Lighthouse

3 **Tater-du** (K4) This unmanned light was established on the cliffs between Porthcurno and Lamorna in 1965, after the loss of a fishing-vessel emphasised the need for a shore light along this stretch of coast.

4 **Wolf Rock** (J1) Wolf Rock, which can be seen from Land's End, was so named because the wind whistling through the rocks resembled the howl of a wolf. The gaps have now been filled in and a waveswept lighthouse tower guards the rock.

5 **Longships** (I2) The first Longships Lighthouse was built on the Carn Bras Rocks off Land's End in 1795. It was a dismal place for the keepers, who were driven demented by the high-pitched noise of the wind between certain rocks. This was improved when a taller tower was built – the first having been engulfed by waves during storms.

6 **Pendeen Watch** (H4) The rugged north coast of the Penwith Peninsula has been the graveyard for many vessels over the centuries. This dramatically sited lighthouse, which is open to the public, can be seen for about twenty miles.

7 **Godrevy Island** (H8) A lighthouse was built on Godrevy Island after the loss of the passenger steamer *Nile* on the rocks of St Ives Bay in 1854. This white octagonal tower is now unmanned.

8 **Trevose Head** (E16) The lighthouse, which is open to visitors, is in a wonderful cliff-top position and can be reached by a toll road. The mid-nineteenth-century tower has a range of twenty-five miles and once had an enormous foghorn eleven metres (thirty-six feet) long.

sunset every day except Sunday or during fog. But the keeper has the right to refuse visitors if other work is in progress.

1 **St Anthony Head** (map ref. M12) St Anthony Head Lighthouse and Pendennis Castle face each other at the tips of the two pincer-like headlands that flank the Carrick Roads off Falmouth. The light guides shipping to the harbour and also gives a warning of the treacherous Manacles to the south. It is open to visitors.

2 **Lizard Point** (O7) Financial difficulties forced the closure of the first lighthouse. A second was opened in 1751, and it is a modified version of this building that stands today, the largest lighthouse in Cornwall, which is open to the public.

Cornwall Coast Path

Cornwall has some of the most spectacular coastal scenery in Britain and there is now a marked path along almost its entire length. The 272 miles of footpath, officially opened in 1973, follow the cliff edge as far as possible, only breaking where towns, estuaries or military installations intervene, or in a few places where rights of way have still not been settled.

The coastline offers a great variety of scenery and has terrain for all types of walker. Some sections are only suitable for the very fit and enthusiastic, while other flatter stretches can be enjoyed by the gentle stroller. Very useful are the Ordnance Survey 1:50,000 scale maps and Bartholomew's half-inch maps, which mark the exact route of the footpath. Here, we can only give a general outline and suggest a few particularly attractive areas.

Spectacular cliff scenery can be found along most of the North Cornwall coast,

Trebarwith Strand

and around the exposed western shores of the Penwith and Lizard Peninsulas. Some stretches of pathway in these areas are remote and quite steep, but the glorious views of the rugged coastline being pounded by the Atlantic rollers are surely worth the effort. There are rough sections between Marsland Mouth and Tintagel, and between Zennor and Cape Cornwall. More gentle stretches of clifftop path can be found between Tintagel and Trebarwith Strand, from Port Isaac to Rock, Padstow to Mawgan Porth, and Lelant to St Ives.

The south coast is generally much softer in character, but no less attractive. The cliffs of the Lizard give way to the wooded hillsides of the Helford River and the estuary of the River Fal. Beyond, the cliffs return and continue as far east as the Devon border, but they are softened by long sandy beaches and by the many fishing villages of this sheltered coastline.

It is difficult to pick out the most outstanding walks, but particularly interesting are the sections from Helford Passage to Maenporth (Falmouth), St Anthony Head to Mevagissey, and Polruan to Polperro.

Kynance Cove

CORNWALL TOURIST BOARD

21

Pendower Beach, Gerrans Bay, near
St Anthony Head

Flowers of Cornwall

Long-leaved scurvy-grass

For many, the spring is the most delightful time to visit Cornwall, when an abundance of wild flowers fills the hedgerows and when the woods are carpeted with bluebells, primroses, wood anemones and wild garlic. The extremely mild and even climate means that spring flowers appear weeks earlier than in other parts of Britain and it also encourages the

Thrift

growth of plants from warmer parts of Europe which are rarely found in Britain. Even sub-tropical plants are able to thrive, and many municipal gardens and the grounds of the stately homes are rich with exotic blooms (see gardens section, pp. 33–5).

The coast is noted for its abundance of wild flowers, many of which are specially adapted to cope with salt spray, and the cliffs, dunes and estuaries all have their special flora. The cliffs, which form much of Cornwall's coastline, support many attractive species, such as thrift, the sea pink that grows here in great profusion. Patches of spring squill, a miniature bluebell, can be found on grassy cliff-slopes in early spring. On the lower cliffs rock samphire is common, with its small yellow flowers and spicy fragrance. Common scurvy-grass, sea campion and tree mallow can be found, together with the colourful Hottentot fig, a naturalised South African plant which hangs in masses on the cliff-face.

The sand-dunes, which mainly occur along the north-west coast, are stabilised by marram grass. Without this solid foundation the shifting sands would stifle other vegetation, such as the lovely sea bindweed with its trumpet-shaped pink flowers, and the most attractive sea holly, which has blue thistle-like flowers

Sea holly

and silver-green prickly leaves. Further inland, where the dunes have become fixed, a greater variety of vegetation can flourish. Common centaury, lady's bedstraw, lesser hawkbit, common birdsfoot trefoil, western eyebright and many other species form a riot of colour in the

Bell heather

Sea aster

spring and early summer. On more shingly beaches the yellow horned poppy, sea sandwort and scentless mayweed will prosper.

Plant life in the estuaries faces the problem of the advancing and retreating tide, and where salt-marshes have developed, they have their own specialised vegetation. Long-leaved scurvy-grass, thrift, sea plantain, sea aster, sea milkwort and sea rush are a few typical Cornish salt-marsh plants.

The cliff-tops and windswept moorland which stretches inland also have an extremely abundant flora, as those who use the Cornwall Coast Path will find out. Both maritime and moorland plants mingle in a rich array of colour. Impenetrable gorse, blackthorn and bramble thickets occur along cliff-tops. Large areas are covered in bracken in summertime, smothering the early spring flowers. Elsewhere heathers are well established, such as ling, bell heather, and cross-leaved heath. The Lizard is a paradise for botanists, with nearly twenty very rare species along the coast and further inland on Goonhilly Downs. This stretch of heathland is vibrant with the golden gorse in early summer. Later, Cornish heath, a very local rare heath, is predominant. Cornwall is also known for an unusual variety of ferns, some of which are very uncommon.

Common gorse

Many rare species are now protected by law, but please resist the temptation to pick even the more common flowers. They won't last long, so are better left to grow where others can enjoy them and where they can seed to grow again another year. Transplanted vegetation is unlikely to survive out of its native habitat.

Birds of Cornwall

The lengthy coastline of Cornwall, with its rugged cliffs and miles of estuary inlets, is a marvellous haven for a wealth of sea birds. The inland area does not have such a variety of birds as other parts of Britain, but local reservoirs and pools attract some interesting species.

Changing patterns of birdlife occur throughout the year, as many birds only spend their winters or summers here, and others make brief visits while migrating. Cornwall is also a common landfall for birds blown off course by storms. These 'vagrants', such as the pectoral sandpiper, may come from as far as North America.

The great variety of Cornish habitats suits many different birds. The cliffs of the north coast are the spring and summer breeding-grounds for many species, including members of the auk family: colonies of guillemots and razorbills are packed on to ledges at scattered locations along the precipitous cliff-walls, and the delightful puffins nest in thousands in burrows on Lye Rock, to the north of Tintagel. Other cliff breeders are the fulmar, with its strange, tube-like nostrils; that excellent fisherman the

Guillemot

cormorant; shags; and many of the gulls, such as the very common herring gull, the great black-backed gull and the kittiwake. After the breeding season many of these species spread out round the coast, move to the estuaries or travel out to sea to their feeding-grounds.

Puffin

A common sight along the rocky shoreline is the striking oystercatcher, with its black and white plumage and bright red beak. Turnstones and purple

Shag

sandpipers can also be seen here, while on sandy beaches a few sanderling pass through during migration.

The Cornish river estuaries are

Kittiwake

favourite spots for bird-watchers, particularly the Camel, Hayle, Tamar, Helford and Fal. The retreating tide leaves vast expanses of mud, much favoured by wading birds and other wildfowl. The birdlife is much richer here during spring and autumn migration, but there will be something of interest at any time of the year. By the Camel estuary is Walmsley Sanctuary, owned by the Cornwall Bird Watching and Preservation Society, where a flock of white-fronted geese winter each year. These can be seen very well from the road.

Typical estuary wading birds are black-tailed godwit, curlew, redshank, knot and dunlin. Ducks also favour the estuaries for part of the year. Shelduck nest in Cornwall, while teal, wigeon, pintail and shoveler winter here. Avocets regularly winter on the Tamar Estuary near Cargreen.

Buzzard

An excellent area for birds on the River Fal lies just below Ruan Lanihorne, and the Truro and Tresillian Rivers, which run through woodland, are also notable. Apart from the presence of waders and ducks, herons have nested here.

One of the richest habitats for birdlife can be found at Marazion Marsh, east of Penzance. A freshwater marsh with reed-beds is separated from the sea by the main road, which provides an excellent vantage point. In summer, reed warblers and water rails occur, and

Dipper

waders are plentiful in spring, but during migration time an extraordinary variety of species passes through. Loe Pool, on the west coast of the Lizard near Helston, is another freshwater pool teeming with birdlife. Stithians Reservoir near Camborne, completed in 1965, is also becoming a popular location.

Inland, Bodmin Moor, Goss Moor and Goonhilly Downs are relatively free from human activity, and birds such as the stonechat, lapwing, golden plover, common snipe and curlew can be found. Other notable inland birds are buzzard, kestrel, raven and magpie, with dipper, grey wagtail and kingfisher occurring along wooded streams.

Food and drink

Traditional Cornish food is becoming very difficult to find, but visitors staying at farmhouses or with local families may be lucky enough to sample the old-fashioned fare. The staple diet of the working people used to be based on fish (particularly pilchards), potatoes and barley flour. From these simple ingredients the inventive Cornish developed a tasty variety of pies, soups, stews and other dishes. For feast days, or whenever it could be afforded, meat or poultry would be added, together with a greater variety of vegetables. Wildlife, such as pheasant, duck and cormorant, also found its way into the kitchen.

Perhaps the best-known food from Cornwall is the pasty. A legend recounts that the Devil never dared advance over the River Tamar into Cornwall for fear of being included in a pasty made by local housewives, who made use of all manner of ingredients in their fillings. The usual mixture is savoury, consisting of chopped-up mutton or steak, potato,

onion and seasoning. Any combination of meat and vegetables can be used, with turnip, swede and leek being popular additions. Pasties can also be sweet, usually filled with apple or some other fruit. One pasty can even include both sweet and savoury at opposite ends – a whole meal in one container. This was particularly useful for the miners or farmers, who needed to take their mid-day meal with them. It is said that pasties did in fact develop in the mining villages and that the pastry shell used to be as hard as rock, so that if the pasty dropped down the mine shaft it did not break! Individual pasties would have the owner's initials at one end and they would be eaten from the other end so that any left-overs could be claimed later. At home, identifying initials are still used so that individual tastes can be catered for, some preferring more turnip or less pepper. Pasties on sale to the public vary enormously in quality and flavour, but the best places to buy them are generally the small bakers or butchers.

The coastal waters of Cornwall still provide an abundance of fresh fish, but the pilchard, once the mainstay of the local diet, is now rarely seen. It was served in a variety of ways; salted, steamed, boiled, marinated, baked, fried, and perhaps most novel of all, as part of star-gazy pie. This culinary delight consisted of pilchards and hard-boiled eggs covered by a pastry crust with slits in it, through which the whole heads of the pilchards gazed skywards.

The thick clotted cream of Cornwall is still a favourite with both residents and visitors alike. It is heaped on pies and pasties, on splits and scones and fried eggs, and it even used to be piled on pilchards. Genuine Cornish ice-cream is also delicious, but quite hard to find. Finally, in the food line, the small local bakeries are worth a visit to sample the bright yellow saffron cake, now quite rare, 'heavy' cake, and cream-filled brandy-snaps, all local specialities.

As for drink, Cornish mead is still manufactured in the county and visitors can sample this potent beverage, made

from fermented honey, at some of the meaderies, such as the one at Newlyn, near Penzance.

Cornwall is an excellent county for attractive country pubs in delightful settings. Many are hundreds of years old and can no doubt boast of local ghosts and lurid tales of ancient murders and smuggling activities. Most of the beer in Cornwall comes from three large breweries: Courage of Plymouth, St Austell Brewery and the Cornish Brewery of Redruth, whose last brewing of Domesday Anniversary Ale, entered in the Excise Book at 11.55 pm on 31 December 1986, not only had the distinction of being the last brew of that year, and in terms of original gravity is probably the strongest beer in the world, but may well yet be proved to possess the greatest percentage alcohol content also. Strong stuff indeed! There are also about one hundred 'real ale' outlets spread throughout the county, including the Blue Anchor at Helston, which actually brews its own beer at the back of the pub.

Historic houses

As you travel down one of the back lanes of Cornwall you may come across the secluded entrance gates to one of the old Cornish manor-houses, with the buildings just visible between the trees. The setting often seems as if it is straight from a Daphne du Maurier novel. Some of these fascinating old family homes and the larger stately homes are open to the public, usually only in the summer and only on certain days of the week, so check locally for opening times.

1 **Antony House** (map ref. N25, off A374 1m. W of Torpoint) This fine example of an early-eighteenth-century house, now owned by the National Trust, was built for Sir William Carew, whose great-grandfather wrote the 1602 *Survey of Cornwall*. The rooms contain an excellent collection of paintings and furniture. The gardens are known for their yew trees and for the Bath Pond House with its plunge bath and elaborate changing-room.

Cotehele House

2 **Cotehele House** (L26, 4m. E of Callington, a turn to the right off A390) The house was built and added to between 1485 and 1627, and for many centuries was owned by the Edgcumbes, an influential Cornish family. The property came into the hands of the National Trust in 1947, complete with many of the original furnishings and a notable weaponry collection. To the south of the house visitors can see the restored manorial water-mill and the adjoining cider-press. At Cotehele Quay the sailing barge *Shamrock* is on view.

3 **Egyptian House,** Chapel Street, Penzance (J5) The flamboyant façade, *c.* 1830, has been restored by the Landmark Trust and the house now belongs to the National Trust.

4 **Godolphin House** (K7, between Godolphin Cross and Townshend, 3m. NW of Breage) The Godolphins were an important local family for many generations and were early investors in the tin-mining industry. The house was later the birthplace of Sydney, 1st Earl of Godolphin, who became Lord High Treasurer to Queen Anne. In the seventeenth century an impressive colonnade was added to the original Tudor house.

5 **Lanhydrock House** (I19, off B3268 2½m. SE of Bodmin) Sir John Robartes, a seventeenth-century tin-mining industrialist, built Lanhydrock House in 1620. The gatehouse and the north wing were the only sections to survive a fire in 1881, but the remainder has since been restored. Of particular note is the original long gallery with its ceiling depicting scenes from the Old Testament. The house, now owned by the National Trust, is set in glorious parkland surrounded by woods where

there are many enjoyable walks and a nature trail. The shrub and formal gardens are also impressive.

6 Mary Newman's Cottage, Saltash (N25) Mary Newman was Sir Francis Drake's first wife, and the cottage, with a central passage and circular staircase to a room above, was probably built in the 1400s.

7 Pencarrow House (H19, off A389 between Wadebridge and Bodmin) An historic Georgian house with an interesting collection of paintings, furniture and china. The extensive grounds include some fifty acres of landscaped formal and woodland gardens, a pets' corner and children's play area.

8 Prideaux Place, Padstow (F18) Set in sixty acres of grounds, which include a deer park dating back to AD 450, Prideaux Place is a beautiful Elizabethan mansion house which boasts a panelled dining-room, the Great Chamber, with an embossed sixteenth-century plaster ceiling. A superb reading-room has panelling and fixtures which originated at Stowe at Kilkhampton, near Bude, which was built by John Grenville, Earl of Bath in 1680, when Charles II was on the throne.

9 Tintagel Old Post Office (E21, in the centre of the village) The National Trust also looks after this unusually small fourteenth-century manor-house with its strangely uneven roof and thick stone walls. In the last century the building was used as a receiving house for letters in the newly established postal service. A room is set up to show a typical Victorian Telegraph Office.

10 Trecarrell Manor, Trebullett, near Launceston (J25) This interesting

place, which can be seen by appointment only, contains a medieval chapel dedicated to St Mary Magdalene and a banqueting hall of the same period with a restored carved roof.

11 **Trerice Manor** (H14, off A3058 about 3m. SE of Newquay at Kestle Mill, well signed) Sir John Arundell, renowned for his defence of Pendennis Castle during the Civil War, built Trerice Manor on the site of an earlier house. Though small, this most attractive building contains fine collections of oak and walnut furniture and of tapestries, and superb plaster ceilings and fireplaces.

Trerice Manor

Gardens

Cornwall's extremely mild climate allows the growth of many plants which will not survive elsewhere in the British Isles and encourages an earlier spring. Many beautiful gardens have been established in the county, taking full advantage of these favourable conditions.

In 1987 the seventy-fifth anniversary of the County Flower Show was celebrated by a Cornwall Gardens Festival which was such a success that it is now an annual event, with nearly seventy gardens open to the public at varying times over an eight-week period during April and May.

1 **Antony Woodland Gardens** adjacent to Antony House near Torpoint (map ref. N25) The woodland garden borders the Lynher estuary and contains fine shrubs, magnolias, camellias and rhododendrons, set in a Humphrey Repton landscape.

2 **Falmouth Gardens** (M11) Falmouth has become nationally famous for its gardens, which contain many exotic flowers, shrubs and trees. The Fox Rosehill Gardens, off Melville Road, Gyllyngdune Gardens and Kimberley Park are all well worth a visit.

3 **Glendurgan Gardens** (M10) The gardens, run by the National Trust, occupy a superb valley site overlooking the Helford River. Visitors can enjoy an excellent maze, walled and water gardens, and a giant's footprint.

4 **Mount Edgcumbe Countryside Park** (O25) The park is situated on a peninsula to the west of Plymouth Sound and can be reached by pedestrian ferry

Glendurgan Gardens

NATIONAL TRUST

and shrubs and plants protected by stone and brickwork, and sheltered by pine trees, tamarisks, *Escallonia euonymous* and other hardy specimens.

7 **Probus, County Demonstration Garden** (K14) A unique education centre has been set up to provide advice on many aspects of garden care, design and productivity. Demonstration gardens show planting techniques. There is also a nature trail, a wildflower collection and an exhibition hall.

8 **Probus, Trewithen Gardens** (K15) An internationally famous collection of camellias, magnolias and rhododendrons and many other rare plants can be seen here, in a wooded and beautifully landscaped setting. Trewithen House, an eighteenth-century country house, is open at certain times of the year.

9 **Trelissick Gardens** (K12) The gardens can be seen in a blaze of colour in springtime, when the rhododendrons, azaleas, camellias and magnolias are in bloom, whereas in the autumn over one hundred varieties of hydrangea provide the main attraction. A nature trail follows the riverside. The gardens are run by the National Trust, but the fine Georgian mansion is not open to the public.

10 **Trengwainton Gardens** (I4, 2½m. NW of Penzance, off A3071) The National Trust also owns these superb gardens, well known for their spring display of rhododendrons and for the great variety of shrubs. Other features include a stream and a walled garden containing delicate plants which are unable to survive in the open elsewhere in England.

from Admiral's Hard, Stonehouse. About thirty-five acres of the extensive parkland are taken up by formal and ornamental gardens. Mount Edgcumbe House is open to visitors at certain times of the year and the park is open daily.

5 **Penjerrick Gardens** (M11) As with many Cornish gardens, spring at Penjerrick is the most rewarding season, with early shrubs in full bloom.

6 **Port Isaac, Long Cross Victorian Gardens** (F20) These gardens with a difference lie in a rugged situation within sight of the Atlantic Ocean and exposed to salt-laden gales. The basis of the gardens is the former Victorian layout, with paths, steps, water, rockeries,

Trelissick Gardens

The church at Altarnun

Churches

Many Cornish churches and towns were named after early Celtic saints before Cornwall came under the influence of the Church of Rome. St Ia gave her name to St Ives, Padstow is derived from St Petroc, and St Neot, St Agnes, St Columba, St Austell and St Piran are just a few of the others whose names have been preserved.

Not many of the early churches remain, but there are some fine medieval examples. The following list is a selection of churches which are notable for their sites or for some outstanding feature, but many villages contain a church or chapel of interest. There are also a number of holy wells and ancient Cornish crosses spread throughout the county. As elsewhere, the numbers and grid references tie in with the maps on pages 60–62.

1 **Altarnun** (map ref. H24) The church at Altarnun, on the northern edge of Bodmin Moor, has one of the highest towers in Cornwall at thirty-three metres (109 feet), giving this church the name, 'The Cathedral of the Moor'. Inside is a fascinating collection of seventy-nine bench-ends, carved in the sixteenth century and depicting aspects of local life.

2 **Roche Chapel** (I17) To the south-east of the village, an unusual outcrop of rocks rises thirty metres (100 feet) above the surrounding plain. A chapel and a hermit's cell are dramatically perched on top of the rocks, from which there is an interesting view over the china-clay countryside.

3 **St Germans** (M24) The superb Norman church at St Germans should not be missed, with its magnificently carved west door and other Norman details. The present church replaced a Saxon cathedral, for until 1030 St Germans was the seat of the original Cornish bishopric, which was moved first to Crediton and then to Exeter.

4 **St Just-in-Roseland** (M12, off the A3078 2m. N of St Mawes) The church lies in an exceptionally lovely setting on a steep wooded hillside overlooking the waters of St Just Creek. The main lych-gate is up on the hillside and the church is reached by descending through a churchyard filled with trees, shrubs and sub-tropical plants. There is a second lych-gate by the water's edge which is often missed by visitors. The interior of this thirteenth-century church is also of interest, particularly for the 500-year-old font, the carved pew-ends and the roof carving.

The west door of St Germans

5 **St Neot** (J21) There is no shortage of legends surrounding St Neot, who is reported to have brought back to life fishes which were mistakenly cooked for him, used wild stags to plough his fields when his oxen were stolen, and carried out various other phenomenal deeds. A superb series of medieval stained-glass windows in the church of St Neot depict some of his activities. The churchyard contains five ancient Cornish crosses.

6 **St Piran's Oratory** (site) (H13, in sand-dunes N of Perranporth) St Piran is also noted for his miracles, not the least of which was having floated from his native Ireland on a millstone, whereupon he built·what was perhaps the first Christian church in England. Unfortunately, drifting sands completely buried it until excavations were carried out in the nineteenth century. Further inundations threatened the site, and a concrete enclosure was constructed to protect this fascinating tiny church, which in recent years has again been completely reburied to ensure its survival. A granite slab now marks the spot and records its history.

St Just-in-Roseland

Castles

Cornish castles were built for two main purposes: the south coast castles, such as Pendennis, St Mawes and St Catherine's, served as a protection against foreign invasion, whereas the inland castles, such as Launceston, were constructed by the Norman invaders to control the local population. Most of the castles are cared for by English Heritage and can be visited daily throughout the year.

Dunheved Castle, Launceston

1 **Dunheved Castle, Launceston** (map ref. H26) As the Norman invaders spread their control over the countryside, they built castles at strategic points, such as Launceston. Dunheved Castle, first mentioned in 'Domesday Book', was the headquarters of Robert de Mortain, half-brother of William the Conqueror. The original fortification consisted of a simple wooden bailey, or protected enclosure, on a motte, or mound of earth. This probably remained until the thirteenth century, when Robert de Cornwall built a stone outer wall, or shell keep. A taller central tower was later added and a roof built between the wall and tower as a fighting-platform. The castle, however, was never heavily attacked, even though Launceston formed a Royalist stronghold in the Civil War. The town and castle surrendered to Fairfax in February 1646 and the fortress gradually fell into disrepair.

2 **Pendennis Castle,** Falmouth (M11) Pendennis Castle was built high on a promontory by Falmouth Harbour in 1543 as part of the coastal defence system constructed by Henry VIII. The estuary of the River Fal and the stretch of water known as the 'Carrick Roads' needed protection against French raiders intent on intercepting local trading-vessels, or planning a full-scale attack on England. The design of the castle contains innovations suited to the change-over of weaponry to the use of cannon. The structure is low, solid and rounded, with splayed gun-ports that could pour shot over a wide angle of the estuary. The castle's defences were eventually put to the test not by foreign invaders, but during the internal struggles of the Civil War. In 1646 Royalists under the stubborn command of Sir John Arundell gallantly held the castle against Parliamentary forces for about five months. An honourable surrender was finally arranged and Pendennis Castle became one of the last Royalist strongholds to fall.

3 **Restormel,** Lostwithiel (J19, 1½m. N of town) Restormel is an example of a Norman motte and bailey castle built in the early years of the Conquest to control a local area. By the late thirteenth century a large stone shell keep replaced the earlier wooden construction. Two-storey buildings encircled the inner

39

courtyard, forming accommodation, storage space, the great hall, a kitchen and military quarters. Edward, the Black Prince, twice visited the castle and spent Christmas here in 1362. Restormel was captured by Royalist troops in 1644. Cromwell later ordered the castle to be slighted (dismantled), leaving the rather attractive ruins that can be seen today. The wall walk offers a superb view of the Fowey valley.

4 **St Catherine's Castle,** Fowey (L19) Only ruins remain of this castle, once a link in Henry VIII's coastal defence system. It was built to guard the entrance to Fowey Harbour, which it did most successfully in 1666 when engaged in action during the wars with the Dutch. It is well worth the walk to the castle, for there is a splendid view of Fowey and the surrounding hills and headlands.

5 **St Mawes** (M12) St Mawes is another castle in Henry VIII's coastal fortification scheme and, together with Pendennis Castle across the Carrick Roads, was built to protect Falmouth's valuable anchorage. It was successful as a sea fort, but easily succumbed to an overland attack during the Civil War, as all its guns faced seawards.

St Mawes

6 **St Michael's Mount** (J6) Rising seventy-six metres (250 feet) out of Mount's Bay off Marazion, this rocky outcrop becomes an island at high tide, but is linked to the mainland by a causeway when the water recedes. The Mount has had a long and violent history since its peaceful early years as a Benedictine monastery founded by Edward the Confessor in 1044. In the twelfth century its potential as a fortress was recognised and in the following 500 years it forcibly changed hands several times during such conflicts as the Wars of the Roses and the Civil War. In 1657 the Mount was purchased by the St Aubyn family, who still live in the castle. The third Lord St Levan presented the island to the National Trust in 1954. Open to visitors on certain days throughout the year.

7 **Tintagel** (E21) A wealth of legend links this spectacularly sited castle with the story of King Arthur. While historians disagree as to whether or not this well-known monarch indeed existed, there is no doubt that he could not have lived in the present castle, for it was built in the twelfth century by Reginald, Earl of Cornwall, the illegitimate son of Henry I. However, it may well have been constructed on the site of an earlier fortification dating back to Arthur's reign, which was probably in about AD 500. The present castle was little used and had fallen into disrepair by the fourteenth century. After strengthening, it served as a prison, but by the sixteenth century it had become a total ruin. The castle was built partly on the mainland and partly on a peninsula. Heavy seas and winds have gradually worn down the connecting isthmus and one day an island will inevitably be formed.

St Michael's Mount

Polzeath

The beach plays an important part in the holidays of most visitors to Cornwall. How many childhood memories must be of the roar of surf, that first plunge into the ocean, the hunt for shells, building fortresses against the incoming tide, endless games of beach football and the inevitable crunch of sand in the lunchtime pasties.

The coast of Cornwall is superbly endowed with beaches for all tastes, from intimate rocky coves to huge expanses of sand and dunes. Some are provided with facilities such as changing-huts, toilets, cafés, shops, car parking, surfboard

Porthminster

rental and bronzed lifeguards. Others may only be reached by walking two miles down a track and descending a steep cliff path, but such coves will probably remain pleasantly deserted.

However safe a particular beach may look, the same cannot be presumed of the sea. Cornwall is notorious for its dangerous offshore currents and the vicious undertows on some beaches, particularly at certain states of the tide. *Warning boards posted on beaches indicate the danger areas. In rough weather red flags are flown when swimming is forbidden.*

Please obey them, or you may risk the life of someone who has to rescue you, as well as endangering your own. Long sandy beaches, such as those in Constantine and Whitsand Bays, can be deceptive for these are both extremely dangerous for swimming.

Glorious surf-riding can be enjoyed on many of the beaches which receive the full force of the Atlantic rollers, mainly those along the north coast. Particularly popular with surfers are Crooklets Beach (Bude), Crackington Haven, Polzeath, Treyarnon Beach (near

Newquay

beaches, usually with gentler waves, which are more suitable for children and weak swimmers, but the waters of the south coast are in general of a calmer nature, except around the west coast of the Lizard. Among the favourite 'family' beaches round the coast are Bude, Harlyn, Treyarnon, Mawgan Porth, Watergate, Newquay, Porthminster (St Ives), Lariggan and Western Beaches (Penzance), Gyllyngvase and Swanpool Beaches (Falmouth), Duporth (Charlestown) and Carlyon Bay.

Padstow), Portreath, Perranporth, Fistral Sands (Newquay), where the World Championships take place, and Porthmeor Beach (St Ives) and Sennen Cove, both Blue Flag beaches.

The north coast also has sheltered

Picturesque coves occur all round the coastline. Those with road access become very crowded in summer, but if you are prepared to walk, deserted coves can still be found. Many occupy indentations in the cliffs and can be reached by steep pathways. Do not stray from the tracks, as Cornish cliffs are extremely crumbly, and rock-climbing is not advised.

Porthgwarra, near Porthcurno

Places to visit

Museums

Many aspects of Cornwall's history have been preserved in numerous museums throughout the county and offer an interesting diversion. They range from large general collections, such as that at the County Museum in Truro, to small specialist exhibitions on smuggling, mining or old agricultural machinery. The large museums are usually open all the year round, but many of the smaller ones are only open during the summer season or on certain days, so check locally for more precise details of opening times. The numbers and grid references tie in with the maps on pages 60-62.

1 **Bodmin** (map ref. I19) *Regimental Museum,* Victoria Barracks. Museum of the former Duke of Cornwall's Light Infantry. Two hundred and fifty years of military history.

2 *Great Western Railway Preservation Society Museum,* Bodmin General Station.

3 *Bodmin Museum.* Local history, natural history, geological and folk exhibits.

4 **Bude** (C26) *Bude-Stratton Historical and Folk Exhibition.* The development of town and canal, mostly in photographs. Features also the numerous ships wrecked off the Cornish coast.

5 **Calstock** (L26) *The Tamar Valley Museum.* A reminder of early shipbuilding on the River Tamar. Old bakery. Exhibits of industrial archaeology.

6 **Camborne** (J9) *Camborne Museum.* Exhibits relating to mining and the life of Richard Trevithick, the Cornish engineer.

7 *Shire Horse Farm and Carriage Museum,* Treskillard (J9, 2m. E of Camborne) Fine collection of period carriages and horse-drawn vehicles. Farming implements. Wheelwright's shop. Horses. Opportunity to ride in an old carriage.

8 **Camelford** (F22) *North Cornwall Museum and Gallery.* Collection of nineteenth-century domestic and farm exhibits. Includes a reconstructed Cornish cottage interior of the 1890s.

9 **Dobwalls** (K22) *Thorburn Museum.* Award-winning museum devoted to the life of Archibald Thorburn, the wildlife artist (1860-1935).

10 **Falmouth** (M11) *Maritime Museum,* Church Street. Many interesting local relics.

11 **Fowey** (L19) *Noah's Ark Folk Museum,* Fore Street. A fifteenth-century house, the oldest in Fowey, holds this excellent museum. The rooms contain sets depicting historical Cornish scenes, such as a merchant's room, photographic studio, wash-house and kitchen, and early diving equipment.

12 **Helston** (L8) *Folk Museum.* Located in the Old Butter Market. Excellent collections of domestic, agricultural, industrial and archaeological exhibits.

13 **Lamanva,** near Falmouth (M11) *Military Vehicle Museum.*

14 **Launceston** (H26) *Lawrence House,* Castle Street. A Georgian house and museum run by the National Trust.

15 *Launceston Rural Museum,* South Petherwin (I25) Seven-acre small-holding with collection of agricultural machinery, vehicles, implements, tools and rural bygones (mostly under cover).

16 **Liskeard** (K22) *Merlin Glass.* Visitors can watch craftsmen at work in the various processes.

17 *Paul Corin Music Museum,* The Old Mill, St Keyne (L22, off B3254 3m. S of Liskeard) Unique gathering of automatic music, including barrel-organs and the Rupfield Violina.

18 **Looe** (M21) *Cornish Museum,* Lower Street, East Looe. Interesting display of arts, crafts, folklore, mining, fishing, witchcraft and superstitions.

19 *Old Guildhall Museum.* Contains gilt maces, pillory stocks.

20 *Lanreath Mill and Farm Museum* (L21, off B3359 7m. NW of Looe) Steam and oil engines, farm implements, clocks, cider-press etc. Various demonstrations.

21 *Trevollard Farm Museum,* Lanreath (L21, off B3359 7m. NW of Looe) Working models of old farm machinery.

22 **Mevagissey** (M16) *Town Museum.* Situated in the original boat-building workshop, built in 1745. Depicts local industries and crafts.

23 **Newquay** (G14) *Trenance Cottages Museum.* Collection of antiques and curios from all over the world.

24 *'Tunnels through Time'.* Exhibition of over seventy full-sized characters portraying Cornish stories and legends.

25 **Padstow** (F17) Museum in the top rooms of *Padstow Institute.* Photographs and nautical exhibits show the maritime history of Padstow.

26 **Penryn** (L11) *Town Hall Museum,* Market Street.

27 **Penzance** (J5) *Museum of Nautical Art,* Chapel Street. Contains four decks of a 1730 man-of-war. Also a display of underwater treasure retrieved from Cornish wrecks.

28 *Museum of the Royal Geological Society of Cornwall,* Guildhall, Alverton Street. Exhibition of local minerals, rocks, fossils and geological maps.

29 *Penlee House Museum and Art Gallery* (off Morab Road). History and development of man in Land's End peninsula. Archaeology, mining, fishing and environment. Permanent collection of paintings of the Newlyn School.

30 **Polperro** (M20) *Smugglers' Museum.* Interesting assortment of items in a village which was notorious for its smuggling connections.

31 **Porthtowan** (I11) *Farm Museum,* Mile Hill. Collection of farm implements, household and dairy utensils, GWR signal box, steam engines, tractors. Replica of GWR engine.

32 **Redruth** (J10) *Camborne School of Mines Geological Museum,* Pool. Collection of rocks and minerals from all over the world.

33 **St Agnes** (H11) *Parish Museum.* A video display and a fascinating collection of pictures, memorabilia, artifacts and exhibits relating to every aspect of the heritage of this parish – the town of St Agnes and its surrounding villages – once an important centre of mining activity.

34 **St Austell** (K17) *Wheal Martyn Museum,* Carthew (2m. N of St Austell on A391) A complete nineteenth-century clay works has been restored to tell the story of the industry. Includes indoor historical display and an introductory audio-visual programme.

35 *Automobilia,* St Stephen (J16) Motor museum of veteran and vintage cars.

36 **St Ives** (H7) *The Town Museum,* at the northern end of the harbour, depicts the local history, industries and traditions, with special emphasis on fishing.

37 *Barnes Museum of Cinematography,* Fore Street. This fascinating museum contains over 1,000 carefully labelled exhibits and traces the evolution of moving pictures. It includes ancient Javanese show puppets, magic lanterns, peepshows and early film cameras.

38 *Barbara Hepworth Museum,* Barnoon Hill. Permanent exhibition of sculpture by the late Dame Barbara Hepworth in her Trewyn studio and garden.

39 **Tintagel** (E21) *King Arthur's Hall,* Fore Street. Built in 1933, this huge stone hall is the headquarters of the Fellowship of the Round Table and depicts many aspects of the Arthurian legend. It also houses ancient manuscripts and Arthurian literature.

40 *Coin Museum,* Fore Street.

41 **Truro** (K13) *The County Museum and Art Gallery,* River Street. Excellent Cornish museum, with special emphasis on the archaeology and general history of

COUNTY MUSEUM, TRURO

Gold collars, *c.* 1800 BC, found at Harlyn Bay and *(centre)* St Juliot

the county. Includes prehistoric weapons and ornaments, a world-famous mineral collection, and displays of Cornish birds and flora. The gallery houses a fine selection of porcelain, pewter, Japanese lacquer, and paintings by well-known artists.

42 **Zennor** (H6) *Wayside Museum of Cornish Crafts.* Displays on mining, quarrying, fishing and agriculture. Housed in an ancient cottage, of which visitors can also see the kitchens and mill with most of its machinery.

Model villages

1 **Goonhavern** (map ref. H13) *World*

St Agnes Leisure Park

in Miniature. Large models of the world's famous statues and buildings in a twelve-acre landscaped garden. Also 'Tombstone', a Western street scene.

2 **Polperro** (M20) *Land of Legend Model Village.* Model village replica of Polperro; animated descriptions of Cornish legends and history, photographic exhibition with commentary, showing old and new Polperro.

3 **St Agnes Leisure Park** (H11) 'Cornwall in Miniature', 'Fairyland', 'Lost World of the Dinosaurs', animated circus. Acres of landscaped gardens.

Railways

1 **Dobwalls Theme Park** (map ref. K22, 3m. W of Liskeard) Miniature steam and diesel engines pull passengers over one mile through attractive woodland scenery.

2 **Lappa Valley Railway,** St Newlyn East (H14, 4m. S of Newquay) A steam locomotive carries passengers on a return trip to the old East Wheal Rose silver and lead mine. The fifteen-inch-gauge railway runs over part of the former GWR line. At the mine site are a boating lake, play area and café.

3 **Launceston Steam Railway** (H26) Steam-haul two-foot-gauge railway using locomotives built over 100 years ago. Stationary steam engines, car and motorcycle museum.

4 **Little Western Railway,** Trenance Park, Newquay (G14) Steam and diesel engines take passengers round a world of miniature stations, bridges and embankments.

5 **Mevagissey Model Railway and International Model Collection** (M16) Nearly fifty trains automatically programmed over extensive layout with detailed scenery. Over 2,000 models of trains from many countries.

6 **The Towans Railway,** near Hayle (I7) Sand-dunes covered with grass provide the setting for this miniature passenger-carrying railway, which runs through several cuttings and a tunnel.

Animal parks

Aquaria Often situated on or near the quayside, such as at East Looe, Fowey, Mevagissey, St Ives and Newquay.

1 **Bodmin Farm Park** (map ref. I20) Friendly animals and display of old farm tools.

2 **Colliford Lake Park Complex** (I22) Sixty-acre park on edge of Colliford Reservoir, specialising in rare and endangered species. Many unusual animals, such as bagot goats and Iron Age pigs.

3 **Cornish Seal Sanctuary,** Gweek (M9) Injured seals washed ashore are cared for in the sanctuary's hospital. The sanctuary is open to visitors all the year round.

4 **Cornish Shire Horse Centre,** Trelow Farm, Tredinnick, Wadebridge (G17) Regular parades of horses, cart rides, working waterwheel, blacksmith and wheelwright at work on site.

5 **Dairyland,** Tresillian Barton, Summercourt (I15) Working farm where visitors can watch 160 cows being milked daily. Farm park with animals, pets

49

and wildfowl. Country life museum, adventure playground.

6 **Killiow Country Park,** Kea, near Truro (K12) Country park and rare breeds sanctuary, gardens, coaching and carriage centre, farm museum, working pottery, spinning and weaving display, carriage rides.

7 **Newquay Zoo,** by Trenance Park (G14) An interesting assortment of animals at this ten-acre zoo.

8 **Padstow Tropical Bird and Butterfly Gardens,** Fentonluna Lane (F17) Tropical birds and plants, plus collections of live and displayed butterflies.

9 **Paradise Park,** Hayle (I7) A seven-acre garden with tropical and rare birds. Also a children's zoo and miniature passenger-railway.

10 **Shire Horse Farm and Carriage Museum,** Treskillard (J9, 2m. E of Camborne) Horses, carriages, etc. See *Museums* (7).

11 **Tamar Otter Park and Wild Wood,** North Petherwin, near Launceston (G26) Wooded park with otters, waterfowl, aviaries, woodland trail with deer, peacocks, pheasant and breeding owls.

12 **Tamarisk Farm Park** on the B3276 coast road between Newquay and Padstow (F16), where friendly young farm animals may be fed and petted, with rare breeds, pony rides and tractor/trailer rides among the other attractions.

13 **Woolly Monkey Sanctuary,** Murrayton, near Looe (M22) The monkeys roam freely in a cliffside rhododendron garden.

Nature trails

1 **The Camel Trail,** Padstow (map ref. F18) to Wadebridge (G19) and Boscarne, near Bodmin (I19), follows the old Southern Region Atlantic Coast Express railway line, now a level trail for walkers, bicycles and horses only, from the open sea at Padstow, beside the lovely Camel estuary, past Little Petherick Creek and Halwyn to Wadebridge and then through delightful woodland scenery, past Grogley to Boscarne.

2 **Coombe Valley** near Bude (C26) One-and-a-half-mile-long trail through a small oak wood and part of a Forestry Commission plantation.

3 **Duchy of Cornwall, Holmbush Picnic Area and Forest Trail** (K17).

4 **The Kit Hill Trail,** Callington (K25) Kit Hill, which rises to 326 metres (1,094 feet) contains much industrial archaeology of the mining era, as well as affording superb views of the surrounding countryside. Its 500 acres were given by HRH The Duke of Cornwall to the county in 1985 for development by the County Council as a Country Park, with a two-mile circular walk and an industrial heritage trail. Car parking access is from the A390, Callington to Gunnislake road.

5 **Poltesco Cadgwith Nature Trail,** Ruan Minor (O8) Circular trail of three miles through valley past caves and cliffs. Interesting rock formations. Remains of serpentine factory.

6 **The Saints' Way** (*Forth an Syns*) from Padstow (F17) to Fowey (L19) This ancient way, now re-opened as a continuous footpath, crosses the Cornish peninsula from the north coast to the

south, using established public paths and minor roads. It re-traces the passage of the Dark Age Christian missionaries through central Cornwall.

Although many of the saints from Ireland and Wales who made the pilgrimage to the shrine of Saint John Compostella in Spain used what is now Lanherne Carmelite Convent at St Mawgan-in-Pydar as one of their stopping places, it is not clear at this distance of time whether they used this way as their direct route across Cornwall to the south coast. What is more probable is that groups of saints used routes in this area as their thoroughfares from which to travel to other parts of Cornwall.

7 **Tehidy Country Park**'s 250 acres of beautiful and varied woodlands, crisscrossed by more than nine miles of footpaths, lie hidden in a sheltered valley between Camborne and the rugged North Cliffs which overlook the Atlantic Ocean (I9). Those footpaths which start at South Drive (free) car park (off a well-signed direct road) are suitable for wheelchairs, and a sensory trail for the visually handicapped also starts at this point. Other free car parks are located at North Cliffs (off the B3301 coast road between Portreath and Hayle) and at East Lodge (near Illogan).

8 **The Tinners' Way,** from Cape Cornwall (H3) to St Ives (H7) is thirteen miles long and, like other old ridgeways of Britain, follows an ancient track or trade route, avoiding valleys where the going would have been tougher and where wild animals might have been encountered. The way is divided into six sections and an illustrated book, with a step-by-step guide and items of interest along the route, is readily available.

Other attractions

1 **Camelot Pottery,** Boscastle (map ref. E22) Visitors can watch hand-thrown studio pots being made and painted. Specialist in Mochaware.

2 **Carnglaze Slate Caverns** (J21, off A38 between Bodmin and Liskeard, 1m. S of St Neot) Disused slate quarry, including an upper chamber ninety-two metres (300 feet) long and a turquoise-coloured underground lake.

3 **Charlestown Shipwreck Centre** (K17) Wreck of the *Grand Turk* displayed to show causes of shipwrecks and the disintegration of wrecks on the sea-bed. Illustrates how finds from wrecks are used to unravel the past.

4 **Cornwall Aero Park, Flambards Victorian Village and 'Britain in the Blitz' exhibition,** Helston (L8) Aircraft, photographic exhibitions, life-size old-world town with carriages, cobbled streets, shops and fashions.

5 **Delabole Quarry** (F21, 4m. S of Tintagel) Visitors can view the 120-metre (400-foot) depth of this gigantic slate quarry from an observation terrace. Also to be seen are slate-splitting demonstrations and a museum.

6 **Frontier City and Museum of the Wild West,** Retallack Park, St Columb Major (H17, near A39) Authentic re-creation of a Wild West city, complete with sheriff's office, saloon and bank.

7 **Goonhilly Satellite Earth Station** (N9) In the middle of the gorse-strewn downland of the Lizard Peninsula, ten giant dish aerials point skywards to pick up signals from

Goonhilly

communications satellites. Automatic audiovisual show, viewing gallery, model of station, tour of site.

8 **Gwennap Pit** (J11, near St Day, 2m. E of Redruth) John Wesley preached at this natural amphitheatre, formed by mine subsidence. Hundreds of Methodists still gather here every Whit Monday, and other services are held during the summer.

9 **Ha'Penny Park,** Wendron (L9) Fun park with circurama, moonshine range, grand prix race-track, bouncing castle and giant elephant, radio-controlled boats and cars, indoor games hall, gardens and video.

10 **John Wesley Shrine** (H24) At Trewint on Bodmin Moor (7m. SW of Launceston), there is a cottage shrine to John Wesley, who stayed here between 1742 and 1762 during his preaching tours.

11 **Land's End** (I2) In addition to the natural attractions of the magnificent cliffs and breathtaking vistas, Land's End now provides a complete day of fascination and family enjoyment. 'The Last Labyrinth', an exciting sound and light spectacular, recalls in vivid detail the days of the Cornish seadogs and smugglers and re-creates the wreck of a sailing vessel, whilst other diversions include 'Man Against the Sea' and 'The Spirit of Cornwall' exhibitions, ship-wreck and boulder play areas, and the Dollar Cove Suspension Bridge, as well as the State House Hotel, with its fine restaurant, bars and conservatory.

12 **Marconi Monument** (M7) On the coast to the west of Goonhilly Downs, above Poldhu Cove, stands a monument to Guglielmo Marconi, who transmitted the first wireless signals across the Atlantic from this site.

13 **Minack Theatre,** Porthcurno (J3, 10m. SW of Penzance) This unique amphitheatre was carved from the cliffs sixty metres (200 feet) above the sea and offers a breath-taking setting for a variety of productions during the summer season, from June to September.

14 **Pixieland Mini-Farm and Pets' Corner,** Kilkhampton (C27) Two and a half acres of various attractions for youngsters.

15 **Pool Winding and Pump Engines** (J10, on A30 2m. E of Camborne) These two enormous beam engines have come under the care of the National Trust and can be visited during the summer. One engine pumped water from a depth of 610 metres (2,000 feet) and the other was used to wind up the tin ore and the miners.

16 **Poldark Mine,** Wendron, near Helston (L9) Explore a Cornish tin mine. Collection of 'bygones', beam-engines.

17 **Tescan Sheepskin Tannery,** Redruth (J10) Guided tours of the tannery.

18 **A World of Nature,** Bude (C26) Natural history exhibition showing local habitats with marine aquaria.

Gazetteer

Space does not allow descriptions of all the towns and villages of this fascinating county, so we have selected those which are most appealing because of their history, buildings, or general attractiveness. Also included are near-by places of interest. Attractions which are described in greater detail elsewhere in the book are highlighted in **bold italic** type. The grid reference after each place name refers to the map on pages 60–62.

Boscastle

Park and ride facilities are provided at Truro, Lelant Saltings for St Ives (by train), Falmouth, Liskeard for Looe (by train), Mevagissey and Fowey during the summer season. A leaflet giving full details is available at Tourist Information Centres.

Bodmin (I19) A pleasant market-town with an ancient history. St Petroc's Church is the largest in Cornwall. *Regimental Museum* and *GWR Museum. Near by: Lanhydrock House; Pencarrow House.*

Bolventor (H22) The Jamaica Inn from Daphne du Maurier's novel is here. *Near by: Dozmary Pool* on Bodmin Moor, where legend claims that King Arthur's sword Excalibur was thrown; *Colliford Lake Park Complex.*

Boscastle (E22) Once an important port, despite the difficult, winding entrance channel, enclosed by steep cliffs. Harbour and surrounding area owned by the National Trust. *Camelot Pottery. Near by:* Superb cliff scenery and stiff walks.

Bude (C26) A spacious resort with huge sandy beaches and excellent surfing. Two swimming-pools, well-organised facilities for tennis, squash, bowls, putting, golf and cricket. Good fishing locally. Canal trail. *A World of Nature. Bude–Stratton Historical and Folk Exhibition. Near by:* Nature trail at *Coombe Valley.*

Callington (K25) Small market-town rivalling Tintagel's claim as the site of King Arthur's Court. *Near by:* Dupath Well, architecturally the most important Cornish holy well; *Kit Hill Trail* for fine views and industrial archaeology.

Calstock (L26) Fishing village and port at the head of the Tamar estuary. The *Tamar Valley Museum* has some interesting shipbuilding and mining exhibits. *Near by: Cotehele House,* and a nature trail from Cotehele Quay.

Camborne and Redruth (J9 and 10) Cornwall's largest urban and industrial area. Old mining centre, with disused chimneys and shafts still very apparent. *Camborne School of Mines* still important *(Geological Museum).* Birthplace of inventor Richard Trevithick. *Camborne Museum. Near by: Pool Winding and Pump Engines;*

Tescan Sheepskin Tannery; Carn Brea (hill with obelisk and marvellous view); Carn Brea Leisure Centre at Pool; *Treskillard Shire Horse Farm and Carriage Museum; Gwennap Pit; Tehidy Country Park* (woodland and walks).

Camelford (F22) An ancient market-town, now a touring centre for North Cornwall. Closely linked with the Arthurian legend, as it is regarded as Camelot. *North Cornwall Museum and Gallery. Near by:* Slaughterbridge, the site of a ninth-century battle, where, supposedly, King Arthur received his mortal wound; Condolden Barrow, 305 metres (1,000 feet) up; Bodmin Moor; *Delabole Quarry.*

Coverack (O9) A traditional Cornish fishing village which used to be most successful in its smuggling activities. The near-by reef, the Manacles, also provided plenty of spoils for the local wreckers.

Falmouth (M11) Developed when Sir Walter Raleigh realised the potential of the Carrick Roads as a huge deep-water anchorage. The port and old town lie on

Falmouth

the river side of the headland and the holiday resort overlooks the English Channel. Even climate all year. Lovely sub-tropical *gardens. Pendennis Castle. Maritime Museum.* Boat trips to Truro. *Near by: Penjerrick Gardens; Glendurgan Gardens;* Helford River; *Lamanva Military Vehicle Museum.*

Fowey from Polruan

Fowey (L19) Lovely old port with a maze of streets and alleys built on the hillside. Sheltered anchorage for yachts. Strong maritime tradition for many centuries. Fowey is the Troy Town of Sir Arthur Quiller-Couch, who lived here. *St Catherine's Castle.* Block-houses. Ferries to Bodinnick and Polruan. End of the *Saints' Way* (from Padstow). *Near by:* Readymoney Cove (bathing); Gribbin Head (National Trust); *Tristan Stone* and *Castle Dore.*

Helford (M10) A truly picturesque village on the Helford River, linked by passenger ferry with Helford Passage. Very congested during the summer.

Helston (L8) The Furry Dance still takes place on each 8 May, when couples dance through the streets throughout the day in an age-old celebration of the arrival of summer linked with the Apparition of St Michael (the town's patron saint). Good centre for visiting the Lizard and Land's End. Interesting *Folk Museum. Near by: Goonhilly Satellite Earth Station; Poldark Mine* and *Ha'Penny Park; Marconi Monument; Loe Pool; Cornwall Aero Park, Flambards Victorian Village* and *'Britain in the Blitz'; Cornish Seal Sanctuary; Godolphin House.*

Kynance Cove (O7) Perhaps the most enchanting of Cornish coves. Interesting rock formations, fine sand, caves, brilliantly coloured serpentine rock, and blow-holes which roar like cannon. Crowded in summer. Toll road.

Lamorna Cove (K4) An artists' colony at the end of a tiny river valley with waterfalls. *Near by:* Bronze Age relics: the *Merry Maidens* and the *Pipers.*

Land's End (I2) This westernmost tip of England is not as spectacular as the cliffs further along the peninsula on each side. 'The Last Labyrinth' and other exhibitions; adventure and play areas; hotel and restaurant. *Near by:* interesting rock formations: Dr Syntax's Head, Dr Johnson's Head, the Irish Lady, and the Armed Knight. The *Longships Lighthouse* is offshore.

Launceston (H26) Ancient market-town dominated by *Dunheved Castle.* Many other historic buildings. *Lawrence House Museum.* St Mary Magdalene Church (remarkably ornate for Cornwall). *Steam railway.* Excellent touring centre. *Near-by: Launceston Rural Museum; Trecarrell Manor.*

Liskeard (K22) An old coinage and stannary town. A Royalist headquarters during the Civil War. King Charles I stayed here for a week. *Merlin Glass. Near by: Dobwalls Theme Park* and *Thorburn Museum; Carnglaze Slate Caverns,* St Neot; Siblyback Reservoir; Cheesewring (moorland rock formation); St Keyne's Well; Tremar Potteries, St Cleer; *Trethevy Quoit; Paul Corin Music Museum.*

Looe (M21) East and West Looe are joined by a seven-arched bridge. Colourful fishing harbour. Narrow streets and alleyways. Centre for shark-fishing. *Old Guildhall* and *Cornish Museums.* Aquarium. Good beaches. *Near by: Woolly Monkey Sanctuary,* Murrayton. Boat trips to St George's Island and along coast.

Lostwithiel (J19) Thirteenth-century capital of Cornwall and a stannary town. Now a pleasant market-town. Centre of activity during the Civil War. A horse was christened Charles in abuse of the King

The vicarage at Morwenstow

in St Bartholomew Church. *Near by:* ***Restormel Castle; Lanhydrock House;*** River Fowey, for keen anglers.

Mevagissey (M16) Pilchards and smuggling used to be the chief interests of Mevagissey residents; now visitors are the mainstay of this charming port. Car park at entrance. Boat trips available. Shark-fishing. Aquarium in the former lifeboat house. ***Town Museum. Model Railway.***

Morwenstow (B27) Parish of the eccentric nineteenth-century poet, the Reverend R.S. Hawker, who built an extraordinary vicarage with chimneys in the shape of church towers.

Mousehole

Mousehole (J5) An attractive little fishing harbour near Penzance, popular with artists and visitors.

Mullion Cove (N7) Tiny harbour, protected by stone jetties. Rival of Coverack in the old smuggling trade. Superb cliff scenery.

Newlyn (J5) To the south-west of Penzance. Known for its artists' community and Orion Gallery. Previously a pilchard-fishing centre.

Newquay (G14) Substantial north-coast holiday resort, offering many sandy beaches and holiday amenities. Excellent surfing. On the headland is the ***Huer's House,*** a look-out post in the days of the great pilchard shoals. ***Trenance Cottages Museum, Little Western Railway*** and ***Zoo. 'Tunnels through Time'.*** Aquarium. *Near by:* ***Trerice Manor.***

Padstow (F18) Attractive north-coast harbour on Camel estuary, named after St Petroc. Linked by ferry with Rock. Full of fishing-boats and yachts. Famed for 'Obby 'Oss Dance on 1 May, an ancient fertility rite in which a man with a huge mask is led round town by the 'Teaser', both followed by singers and dancers. ***Prideaux Place. Maritime Museum. Tropical Bird and Butterfly Gardens.*** Start of the ***Camel Trail*** (to Wadebridge and Bodmin) and the ***Saints' Way*** (to Fowey). *Near by:* Good beaches at Trevone, Harlyn, Treyarnon; ***Trevose Head Lighthouse; Tamarisk Farm Park.***

Penzance (J5) Retains its attractive market-town flavour despite the influx of tourists. Western terminus for the railway. Sports and entertainment.

Padstow

Penzance

Excellent touring centre for the Penwith Peninsula. Ferry service to Scilly Isles leaves from harbour. Mild climate encourages beautiful sub-tropical gardens. *Museum of Nautical Art. Royal Geological Society Museum. Penlee House Museum and Art Gallery. Near by: St Michael's Mount; Trengwainton Gardens;* Newlyn; *Marazion Marsh* (for birds).

Perranporth (H13) A modern holiday resort with an extensive sandy beach, good surfing and many amenities. *Near by: St Piran's Oratory* (buried in sand-dunes); Perran Round (ancient amphitheatre); *World in Miniature,* Goonhavern.

Polperro (M20) Perhaps the most picturesque Cornish fishing village, packed tightly into a cleft in the cliffs, with a stream running by the main street. Damaged by floods in 1976, but rebuilt. Traffic-free, but congested by summer visitors. *Smugglers' Museum.* Craft shops. Artists. *Land of Legend Model Village.*

Port Isaac (F20) Steep hills lead down into the small fishing village with its tightly packed houses. *Leave your car outside the village.*

Prussia Cove (K6) An eighteenth-century smuggler, known as the 'King of Prussia', operated out of this cove. Now popular for diving and fishing.

St Agnes (H11) Formerly a tin-mining and fishing centre, now developing as a tourist spot. Ruined engine-houses all around. *Parish Museum. Model village.* Good beaches and surfing. *Near by:* St Agnes Head, with its disused lighthouse; superb coastal views; Trevaunance Cove; *Porthtowan Farm Museum.*

St Austell (K17) Centre of the china-clay industry. Huge mounds of waste material lie near the town. Polkyth Leisure Centre. *Near by:* good beaches and modern facilities at Carlyon Bay and Duporth Beach; *Wheal Martyn Museum; Automobilia.*

St Columb Major (H16) Ancient market-town notable for its church and the tradition of Cornish hurling with a silver ball, played twice during Shrove-tide. *Near by: Castle-an-Dinas* (early fort); Nine Maidens, and the Fiddler; *Frontier City and Wild West Museum.*

St Ives (H7) Despite commercial-isation, this busy fishing village retains its charm. Steep, cobbled streets and

Port Isaac

closely built houses surround the quayside. Still a Mecca for artists. **Barnes Museum of Cinematography.** Craft centre. **Barbara Hepworth Museum. Town Museum.** Good restaurants. Several excellent beaches (Porthmeor a favourite with surfers). Church of St Ia. Start of the **Tinners' Way** (to Cape Cornwall).

St Mawes (M12) Attractive little port and boating centre on the Roseland Peninsula, linked by ferry to Falmouth. **St Mawes Castle** was built at the same time as Pendennis, across the Carrick Roads. Good views. *Near by:* **St Just-in-Roseland Church; St Anthony Head Lighthouse.**

Stratton (D26) Boasts an interesting parish church with a fine tower. For many centuries it was a busy market-town with a full complement of traders and craftsmen and it was not until the latter half of the nineteenth century, as Bude developed as a seaport, that Stratton began to lose status. A Town Trail leaflet is now available to guide visitors through the maze of fascinating streets and alley-ways. *Near by:* Stamford Hill, the site of an historic and important battle during the Civil War; Stowe, home of Sir Bevil Grenville and his manservant, Anthony Payne, the Cornish Giant figured prominently.

Tintagel (E21) Popular centre for those interested in legends of King Arthur and his **castle,** which is now a romantic cliff-top ruin. In the village are **King Arthur's Hall** (museum), fourteenth-century **Old Post Office, Coin Museum,** ancient church.

Truro (K13) County administrative centre and cathedral city at the head of the Truro River. Some corners retain the flavour of the old seaport. The cathedral was completed in 1909. Absorbing **County Museum.** Boat trips to Falmouth. Good shopping centre. *Near by:* **Killiow Country Park, Kea.**

Wadebridge (G19) A 500-year-old, many-arched bridge crosses the head of the Camel estuary in Wadebridge, once a medieval port. Home of the Royal Cornwall Show in early June. The **Camel Trail** passes through the town. *Near by:* **Pencarrow House; Cornish Shire Horse Centre, Tredinnick.**

Zennor (H5) A bleak moorland village just off the Land's End to St Ives coast road. Famous **mermaid bench-end** in church. Excellent **Wayside Museum of Cornish Crafts.** Tinners' Arms Inn. *Near by:* **Zennor Quoit** (cromlech); **Men-an-Tol; Chysauster** (Iron Age village); magnificent coastline.

Truro

Key to symbols	page		
🏛 Prehistoric monuments	5	**CF**	Car ferry
🗼 Lighthouses	19	**PF**	Passenger ferry
🏠 Historic houses	30	**PR**	Park and ride
✲ Gardens	33	⊕	Airport
♗ Churches	37		
🏰 Castles	39		
🏛 Museums	46		
🕍 Model villages	48		
🚂 Railways	49		
� Animal parks	49		
❗ Nature trails	50		
☆ Other attractions	51		

To read about the various numbered castles, gardens, etc. on this map, look at the key, turn to the appropriate page and find the corresponding numbered item.

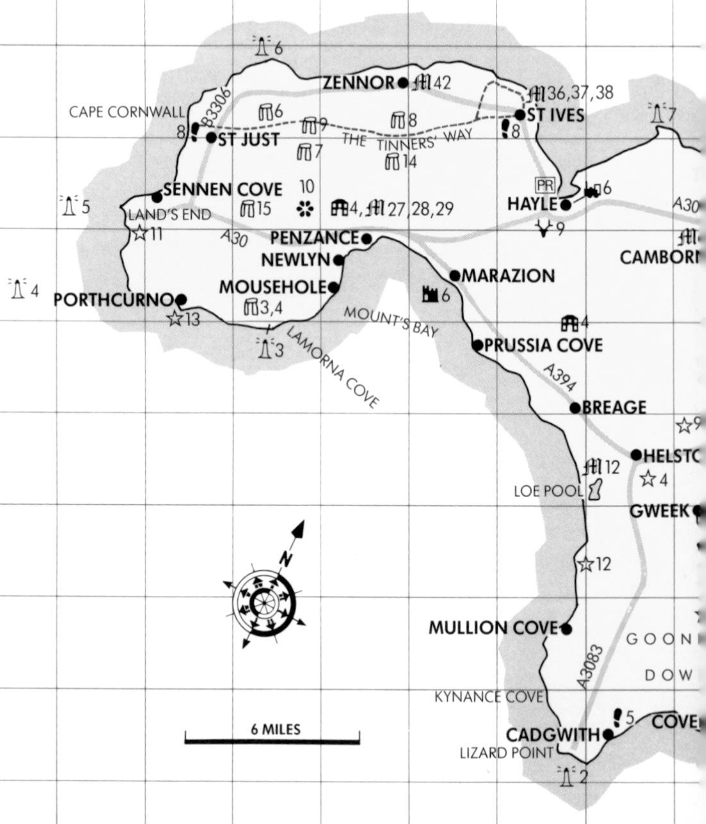

🗼 6

ZENNOR ● 🏛42   🏛36,37,38

CAPE CORNWALL   🏛6   🏛9   🏛8   ●ST IVES   🗼 7

8 ●ST JUST   🏛7   THE TINNERS' WAY   🏛8

B3306   🏛14

🗼 5   SENNEN COVE   10   PR   🏛6

LAND'S END   🏛15   ✲   🏠4, 🏛27,28,29   HAYLE●   A30

☆11   A30   PENZANCE●   ⳷9   🏛
NEWLYN●   CAMBORN

🗼 4   MOUSEHOLE●   ●MARAZION

PORTHCURNO●   🏛3,4   🏠4

☆13   LAMORNA COVE   MOUNT'S BAY   🕍6   ●PRUSSIA COVE

🗼3   A394   A394

●BREAGE   ☆9

●HELSTO
🏛12   ☆4
LOE POOL   GWEEK●

☆12

MULLION COVE●   GOON

D O W

KYNANCE COVE   A3083

❗5   COVE
6 MILES   CADGWITH●
LIZARD POINT   🗼 2

60

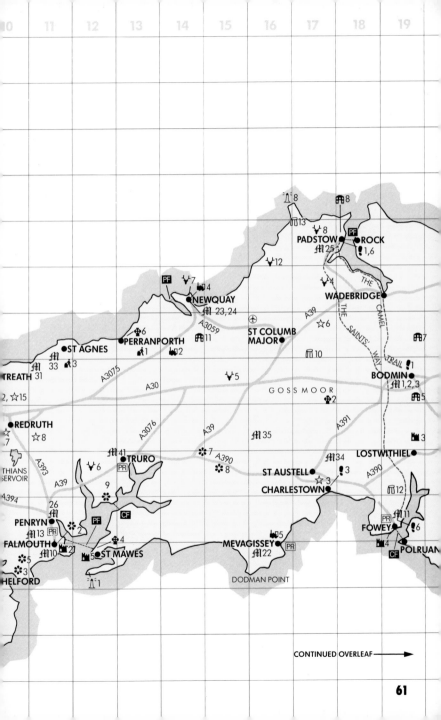

⛺8

🏛8

🏛13

☽8 PR ROCK
PADSTOW ▮1,6
🏠25

☽12

☽4 WADEBRIDGE

PF ☽7
🏠4 NEWQUAY
🏠23,24

A3059

✈

🏠11 ST COLUMB
MAJOR

🏛10

✝6
PERRANPORTH
🏚1 🏠2

●ST AGNES
🏠33 ⛄3

🏠 31
TREATH

A3075

A30

✿5

☆6

🏛7

BODMIN●
🏠1,2,3
🏛5

GOSSMOOR

✝2

☆15

2,

●REDRUTH
☆8
☆7

A3076

A39

🏠35

A391

⛺3

LOSTWITHIEL●

✿7 A390
✿8

🏠34

ST AUSTELL●

CHARLESTOWN●

✝3
▮3

🏛12

🏠41
PR TRURO
✿6

9

✿

A394

26
🏠
PENRYN●
🏠13 PR
FALMOUTH●
🏠10 🏚1

CF
PF

⛄4
🏚5 ●ST MAWES

MEVAGISSEY
🏠22 PR

🏚5

✿5

⛺1

PR 🏠11
FOWEY●
▮6

🏚4
CF POLRUAN

⛄5

⛄3
HELFORD

DODMAN POINT

CONTINUED OVERLEAF⟶

THIANS
ERVOIR

A39

A393

MORWENSTOW

☆14 KILKHAMPTON

!2

BUDE ☆18
𝔐4
WIDEMOUTH BAY ●STRATTON
A3072

CRACKINGTON HAVEN

𝔐39,40
☆1
⚑7 BOSCASTLE
TINTAGEL
⚑9

❋6
PORT ISAAC
☆5

𝔐8
CAMELFORD

A39

A395

✠11

ALTARNUN ●⚕1
BOLVENTOR ☆10
🏛1
LAUNCESTON
🏛3 𝔐14
⚑1
𝔐15

A30
✠2 BODMIN MOOR

𝔐1,2,3
BODMIN
🏛5 ✠1

A38
⚑5
ST NEOT
🏛2
☆2
🏛10

𝔐9
⚑1 🏛5
16𝔐 LISKEARD
PR
𝔐17
CALLINGTON !4 A390

𝔐15
CALSTOCK
🏛2

𝔐20,21
POLRUAN
⚑2 𝔐30
POLPERRO● LOOE● ✠13
A38
✠3
ST GERMANS
𝔐18,19
🏛6 A38
TORPOINT

🏛1,❋1

WHITSAND BAY

●PLYMOUTH
CF

❋4

RAME HEAD

62

DEVON

RIVER TAMAR

Index